It's called a warren.

A fox's home

Foxes make a home underground.
The home has a special name.

Animal homes

CONTENTS

A rabbit's home..................................2

A fox's home.....................................4

A badger's home 6

A squirrel's home 8

An otter's home 10

Other animal homes 12

Index..16

A rabbit's home

fur

Rabbits make a home underground.
The home has a special name.

2

bare soil

It's called an earth.

A badger's home

Badgers make a home underground.
The home has a special name.

straw and leaves

It's called a sett.

A squirrel's home

twigs and grass

Squirrels make a home in a tree.
The home has a special name.

It's called a drey.

An otter's home

Otters make a home in a river bank.
The home has a special name.

grass and moss

It's called a holt.

Other animal homes

A mole's burrow

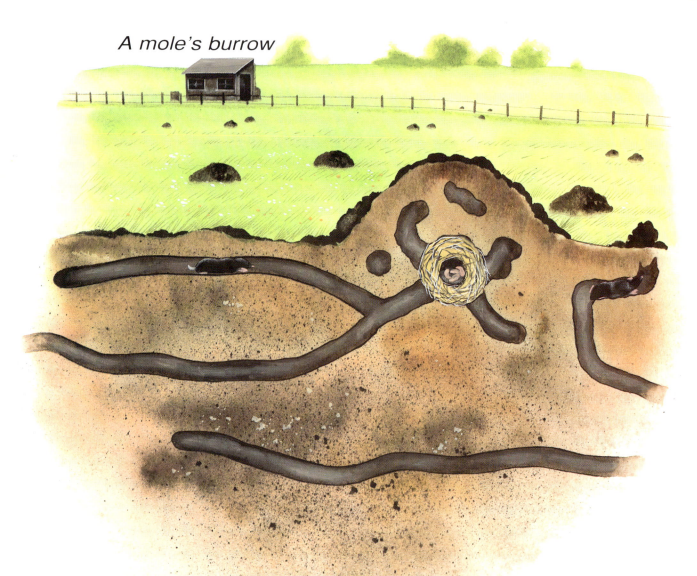

Here are some more animal homes.

A hedgehog's nest

Find the animals and their homes.

1 rabbit
2 warren
3 hedgehog
4 nest

5 otter
6 holt
7 badger
8 sett

9 squirrel
10 drey
11 fox
12 earth

Index

badger.....................6

drey.........................9

earth.......................5

fox...........................4

holt.........................11

otter......................10

rabbit.....................2

sett.........................7

squirrel..................8

warren...................3